Why Science Matters

Harnessing the Sun's Energy

Andrew Solway

Heinemann Library
Chicago, Illinois

Customer Service 888-454-2279
Visit our website at www.heinemannraintree.com

Editorial: Andrew Farrow, Megan Cotugno, and Harriet Milles
Design: Steven Mead and Q2A Creative Soultions
Illustrations: Gordon Hurden
Picture research: Ruth Blair
Production: Alison Parsons

Originated by Modern Age
Printed and bound in China by Leo Paper Products

ISBN: 978-1-4329-1834-7 (hc)
ISBN: 978-1-4329-1847-7 (pb)

13 12 11 10 09
10 9 8 7 6 5 4 3 2 1

Library of Congress Cataloging-in-Publication Data
Solway, Andrew.
 Harnessing the Sun's energy / Andrew Solway. -- 1st ed.
     p. cm. -- (Why science matters)
 Includes bibliographical references and index.
 ISBN 978-1-4329-1834-7 (hc) -- ISBN 978-1-4329-1847-7 (pb)
 1. Solar energy--Juvenile literature. I. Title.
 TJ810.3.S63 2008
 333.792'3--dc22
                        2008014356

Acknowledgments
The publisher would like to thank the following for permission to reproduce photographs:
©Alamy (Clynt Garnham) **p 29**; ©Corbis **pp 21**, **44** (Brooks Kraft), **6** (Michael St. Maur Sheil), **38** (Michael Macor/San Francisco Chronicle); ©Getty Images **pp 46** (Denis Doyle), **32** (Popperfoto);©NASA **p 8**; ©Photodisc/StockTrek **pp 4**, **33**; ©Science Photo Library **pp 26** (Alex Bartel), **24** (Martin Bond), **17** (Martyn F. Chillmaid), **45** (Lynette Cook),**34** (Colin Cuthbert), **35** (Dryden Flight Research Center Photo Collection/NASA, **18** (Gusto Images), **39** (Laguna Design), **23** (Pat & Tom Leeson), **9** (Simon Lewis), **15** (NASA), **27** (NREL/ US Department of Energy), **30** (Scott Sinklier/AGSTOCKUSA). Background images supplied by ©istockphoto.

Cover photograph of the Sun reproduced with permission of © Corbis/Lester Lefkowitz. Background image supplied by ©istockphoto.

The publishers would like to thank David Ockwell for his invaluable assistance in the preparation of this book.

Every effort has been made to contact copyright holders of any material reproduced in this book. Any omissions will be rectified in subsequent printings if notice is given to the publishers

Contents

Some words are printed in bold, **like this**. You can find out what they mean in the glossary.

Why Do We Need to Know About the Sun?

On January 20, 2005, there was a huge explosion on the surface of the Sun. The power of it was incredible—like 20 million atomic bombs all going off at once. The blast hurled billions of tons of super-hot, electrically-charged gas many miles into space.

Solar flare

Huge explosions like this happen quite often on the Sun's surface. They are called **solar flares**. Scientists have studied solar flares for many years, using telescopes and space satellites. Solar flares sound exciting, but do we really need to study them? How does something happening 150 million km (93 million miles) away affect us here on Earth?

In fact, solar flares can affect Earth. Large flares produce clouds of very high-energy particles called proton storms. Protons are very tiny, positively charged particles that are parts of **atoms**. Proton storms can reach Earth, where they damage communications and electronic equipment.

Powerhouse

Solar flares are just a tiny part of the incredible energy output of the Sun. This energy is essential to most processes that happen on Earth. Without it, Earth would be a bare, dry, lifeless rock.

Solar flares can send a tongue of flame millions of miles into space. Sometimes the flare loops around, back to the Sun's surface.

Spots and space weather

For nearly 3,000 years, astronomers have been fascinated by sunspots, which are small spots on the Sun's surface. They soon noticed that the sunspots do not always stay the same. Sunspot numbers change in a regular, repeating cycle. Every 11 years, sunspot numbers reach a maximum, then reduce suddenly.

In 1852, British astronomer Edward Sabine (1788–1883) and others noticed that there was a connection between sunspot numbers and changes in Earth's magnetic field. It was the first evidence that events on the Sun influence what happens on Earth. There is some evidence that large sunspots affect our weather. Earth's climate is warmer when there are large numbers of sunspots, and colder when there are fewer.

This graph shows how sunspot numbers have changed over the last 400 years. During the time known as the Maunder Minimum, the weather on Earth was especially cold. The period of the Dalton Minimum was cold, too.

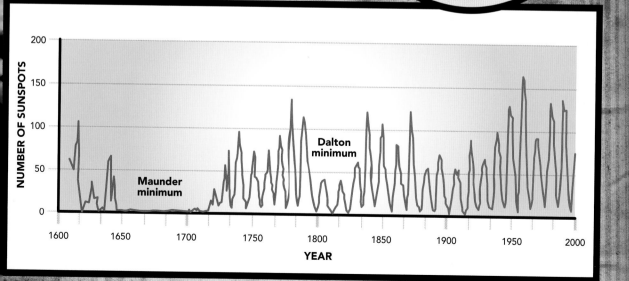

A growing need for energy

The Sun supplies enough energy to light and heat Earth, to keep life going, and to power the weather, ocean movements, and other processes. However, in the modern world we need energy for other things, too, such as heating homes and offices, powering cars and other vehicles, and producing electricity in power plants. Most of this energy comes from **fossil fuels**, which are oil, gas, and coal.

The amount of energy we need each year is always growing. This is partly because the world's population is growing. It is also partly because the world is changing. More and more countries are becoming **industrialized**, producing goods in factories rather than farming to grow food. Industries need a lot of energy, so energy use keeps growing.

On this oil-drilling platform, gas that is mixed in with the crude oil is burned off as waste. It would save energy to capture the gas and use it as fuel.

The energy crisis

For many years, the growing use of energy did not seem to be a problem. There were always new coal deposits and oil fields to find. Experts do not agree about how long fossil fuels will last. Oil supplies could run out in less than 50 years, gas may last a little longer, and coal could last 200 years. However, long before they run out altogether, the amount of fossil fuel we can produce will start to fall. We will not be able to produce enough energy from fossil fuels for all our needs.

Climate change

Most scientists agree that the gases produced by burning fossil fuels are causing **climate change**. Overall, the world is getting warmer. The ice at the North and South Poles is melting, causing sea levels to rise. Some places could become flooded. In warmer areas, higher temperatures and less rainfall are turning farmlands into desert. There are now more weather extremes. Hurricanes, floods, and droughts are becoming more severe.

This graph shows the increase in carbon dioxide concentration in Earth's atmosphere and the rise in global temperature since 1750. It also forecasts the temperature changes up to the year 2100, if we continue to burn fossil fuels at our current rate of consumption.

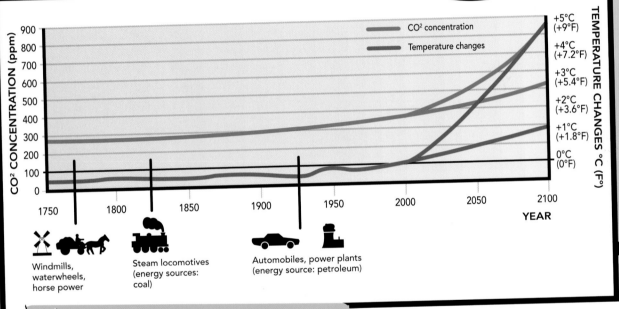

Windmills, waterwheels, horse power

Steam locomotives (energy sources: coal)

Automobiles, power plants (energy source: petroleum)

THE SCIENCE YOU LEARN: THE SUN'S ENERGY

The Sun produces a massive amount of energy. It gives out almost 400 billion billion megajoules (95.5 billion billion megacalories) of energy per second. About 800 billion megajoules (190 billion megacalories) of this energy reaches Earth every second. This is about 8,000 times as much energy as we use in a year. If we could harness even 1/1,000th of this energy, it would be more than enough to supply all our energy needs.

What can we do?

To solve the world's energy crisis, we need to a) reduce the amount of energy we use, and b) find ways to generate "clean" energy, which does not produce greenhouse gases and will not run out. Could the Sun provide us with clean energy? Can we harness its enormous power and help solve our energy crisis?

Hot, Hot, Hot!

We all know the Sun is hot, but exactly how hot is it? Where does the heat come from? How does it travel 150 million km (93 million miles) to reach Earth? Scientists can tell from the color of the Sun (see box) that the temperature at the surface is around 6,000°C (10,830°F). This is about twice as hot as the filament in a light bulb, and more than four times as hot as a steel furnace. However, the Sun is far hotter at its center. This is where all the Sun's energy is produced.

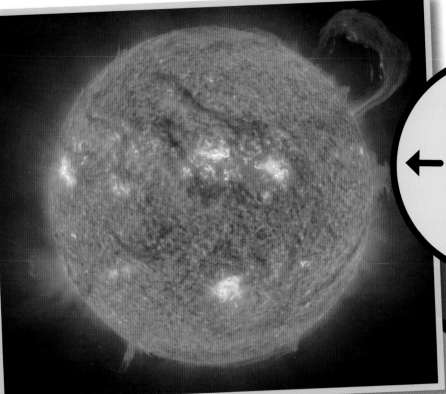

The Sun is a huge ball of hot gas. You could fit 109 Earths across the Sun's diameter, and its volume is over one million times greater than that of Earth.

Giant gas ball

The Sun is made mostly from hydrogen gas, plus some helium, and tiny amounts of other materials. Hydrogen and helium are the two lightest gases in the universe, so the Sun's **density** is only about one-quarter of Earth's. However, the Sun is so huge that it still weighs an enormous amount. It is more than 330,000 times heavier than Earth, and 500 times heavier than all the planets and other objects in the solar system put together.

The Sun's nuclear power

The hydrogen at the center of the Sun is under a huge amount of pressure from the weight of the gas above it pushing down, and it gets tremendously hot. The conditions at the Sun's center cause a **nuclear reaction** known as **nuclear fusion** (see page 42). This is different from the type of nuclear power we use to generate electricity. The fusion reaction is like a continuous atomic explosion going on in the heart of the Sun. It raises the temperature to over 13 million°C (23.4 million°F). This is the source of the Sun's power.

This heated iron rod shows how the color a material glows changes with temperature. The white area of the rod is the part that is hottest. The red area is cooler.

THE SCIENCE YOU LEARN: COLOR-CODED TEMPERATURE

If you heat up the end of a metal poker in a fire, it begins to glow a dull red. If you heat it more, for example in a furnace, it will glow orange, then yellow, then white hot.

In 1893, German physicist Wilhelm Wien (1864–1928) showed that this common observation was actually an example of a physical law. He worked out that in an ideal situation, the temperature of a material is directly related to the **wavelength** of the light it gives off. The Sun is close to ideal in the way it gives off light. By analyzing the light given off by the Sun, it is possible to work out the temperature at the surface.

A million-year journey

The energy generated in the center of the Sun has a long journey to reach Earth. It travels out from the center in two ways. Initially, the energy travels as radiation. The particles in the Sun's center give out very high-energy waves called radiation. However, the radiation does not travel far, because the particles in the center and middle layers are packed so close together. The radiation hits another particle, which absorbs the energy, then emits it again. This new high-energy wave travels only a tiny distance before it too is absorbed, and so on. The radiation itself travels at the speed of light, but the energy travels out from the center to the outer layers of the Sun very slowly. It can take thousands or millions of years for the energy from the center to reach the outer layers of the Sun.

In the outer layers, the gas is less dense than near the center. It acts more like a fluid, moving and swirling around. Once energy from the center gets this far, it travels by **convection**. This takes much less time than it takes to get through the inner part of the Sun.

THE SCIENCE YOU LEARN: HOT PARTICLES

A large amount of the energy that the Sun produces is heat. The hotter the Sun gets, the more energy it has. The energy is to do with the movement of its particles.

The particles that make up any substance are never still. In a solid, they just vibrate back and forth. With more energy, a solid becomes a liquid, and the particles begin to slide over each other. With more heat, the liquid becomes a gas, and the particles have enough energy to escape from each other altogether and fly through space.

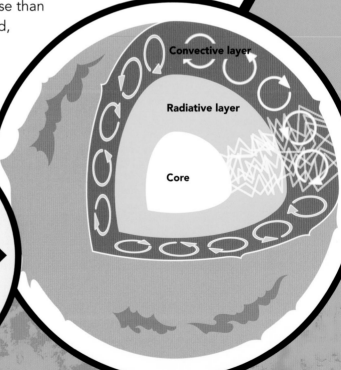

Convective layer

Radiative layer

Core

The diagram shows the structure of the Sun. The central core is hot and very dense. The radiative layer and the convective layer are cooler and less dense than the core.

Eight-minute journey

The surface of the Sun is called the photosphere. From here, the energy is radiated out as light. There are layers of gas beyond this called the corona (the Sun's atmosphere), but they are transparent to light. The light radiates out through this layer and into space. The journey from the Sun's surface to Earth takes just eight minutes.

Conduction, convection, and radiation are the three ways that heat can be transferred from one place to another.

Convection

Conduction

Radiation

THE SCIENCE YOU LEARN: HEATING THE HOUSE

Heating a building relies on convection and radiation. When you first turn on a heater in a cold room, you can feel the heat from it, even though the air around you is cold. The warmth you feel radiates out from the heater. After the heater has been on for a while, the air in the room warms up. This happens partly through convection. Warm air close to the heater rises, and cooler air from farther away moves in to take its place. The air in the room begins to move in a large circle, rising as it is warmed near the heater, and sinking as it cools farther away from the heater.

INVESTIGATION: HEAT TRANSFER

There are three main ways in which heat can transfer from one place to another. They are conduction, convection, and radiation. The investigations below demonstrate each of these processes.

1. CONVECTION

Equipment
- ice cube tray
- food coloring
- water
- freezer
- large jar or dish
- hot water

Convection currents in water

Procedure
Make some ice cubes from food coloring mixed with water. Fill a large jar or dish with hot water, then add one of the colored ice cubes. Observe what happens to the coloring.

2. CONDUCTION

Equipment
- paraffin wax
- thumbtacks
- metal rod
- Bunsen burner

Conduction in a metal rod

Procedure
Using the paraffin wax, attach the thumbtacks at regular intervals along the rod. Heat one end of the rod using the Bunsen burner.

Watch carefully what happens to the thumbtacks. Do they fall off? Which one falls off first?

Thumbsticks stuck to metal rod with paraffin wax

Bunsen burner

3. RADIATION

Equipment
- paraffin wax
- two thumbtacks
- two small metal squares, one black, one silver
- two clamp stands
- Bunsen burner

Procedure
Using the paraffin wax, attach a thumbtack to the back of each metal square. Clamp a metal square on each clamp stand. Light the Bunsen burner and position the squares on either side of it.

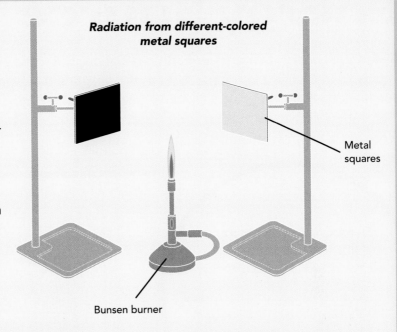

Radiation from different-colored metal squares

Metal squares

Bunsen burner

Observe the experiment until one of the thumbtacks falls off. Which one falls off first? How is this different from the conduction experiment?

Results

1. In the convection experiment, the coloring in the ice cube is slowly released as the ice cube melts. The movement of the coloring through the water shows the convection currents in the water.

2. In the conduction experiment, the thumbtacks fall off one by one as the metal rod heats up and melts the paraffin wax holding them in place. The metal rod first becomes hot near to where it is being heated, and the heat is gradually conducted along the rod.

3. In the radiation experiment, the two metal squares are heated mainly by radiation. The paraffin wax melts as the metal squares heat up, and the thumbtacks fall off. The thumbtack on the black square should fall off first, because black objects are good at absorbing and emitting heat, while white or silver objects are good at reflecting heat.

Understanding conduction, convection, and radiation is important for any manufacturer making heating equipment, or for someone deciding how to heat a space. For example, in a wood-burning stove, heat from the fire is conducted to the outer surface of the stove, because it is made of metal. The stove is painted black so that it is a good radiator of heat. Finally, the air above the stove is heated most and rises as it becomes warmer than the surrounding air. Cooler air moves in to replace it, creating a convection current.

Sunlight as an Energy Source

All the Sun's energy that reaches Earth is radiation. This is the only way that energy can travel through space. Most of the radiation that comes from the Sun is visible light. There are also some other kinds of radiation, such as high-energy X-rays and lower-energy infrared radiation. However, most of these types of radiation are absorbed by Earth's atmosphere.

This graph shows that most of the Sun's radiation is in the visible range, with smaller amounts of infrared and ultraviolet radiation. The difference between the yellow area and the red areas shows the radiation that is absorbed by the atmosphere.

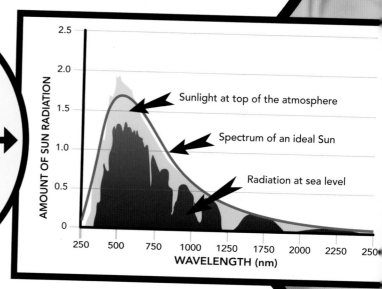

Sunlight at top of the atmosphere

Spectrum of an ideal Sun

Radiation at sea level

From light to warmth

When sunlight reaches Earth, some of it is reflected from objects on the surface. This reflected light is what our eyes pick up—it is how we see things. However, large amounts of light are absorbed rather than reflected. When a substance absorbs light or another type of energy, the particles in the substance gain energy, and they begin to move more quickly. In other words, the substance gets warmer. When the substance becomes warmer than its surroundings, it passes on some of the warmth to the surrounding air by radiation and convection. This is how sunlight warms Earth.

Different surfaces and materials absorb different amounts of sunlight and heat up the air around them by different amounts. Dark rock, for example, absorbs more sunlight than light-colored rock. This means that different parts of the atmosphere are heated by different amounts. This uneven heating causes convection currents in the air. Where the air is warmer it rises, and cooler air flows in to take its place. We feel this air flow as wind.

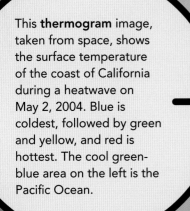

This **thermogram** image, taken from space, shows the surface temperature of the coast of California during a heatwave on May 2, 2004. Blue is coldest, followed by green and yellow, and red is hottest. The cool green-blue area on the left is the Pacific Ocean.

Hot light

When an object radiates heat, it produces a type of radiation known as **infrared**. In 1800, infrared radiation was discovered by astronomer William Herschel (1738–1822). He had been looking at the Sun using colored filters to cut out most of the light, so that his eyes would not be damaged. While he was using the filters, he noticed that some of them seemed to let through warmth, while others did not.

Herschel did several experiments to test the temperature of different parts of the **spectrum** of sunlight. He found that the red end of the spectrum was warmer than the blue end. During one experiment, he came back after a break to find that the Sun had moved across the sky, and his measuring thermometer was in the dark region beyond the red end of the spectrum. To his surprise, he found that this dark region was warmer than any part of the visible spectrum. He concluded that there must be another kind of radiation, invisible to our eyes, in addition to the light we can see. This is what we now call infrared radiation.

Other transformations

Sunlight can transform into other kinds of energy besides heat. Plants absorb sunlight and turn it into food. The energy from sunlight is used to drive chemical reactions in the plants. We will learn more about this process (photosynthesis) on page 20.

Energy transformations are a basic part of most things that do useful work. Matches, for example, have chemical energy stored in the chemicals of the match head and the wood. When you strike the match, friction makes the match head flare up, and this starts the wood burning. The chemical energy stored in the match is turned into heat.

A car engine makes two energy transformations. First, it turns chemical energy into heat. This happens in the cylinders of the engine, where the fuel is mixed with air and burns in a sudden explosion. Then the heat energy is turned into **kinetic energy** (motion). This happens because the explosion of the fuel causes the gases inside the cylinder to expand. The expanding gases push on a piston in the cylinder and make it move.

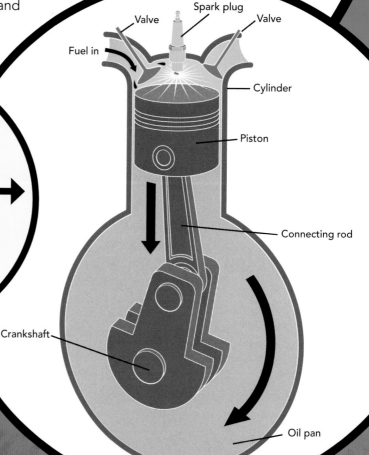

This diagram shows how a car engine works. Chemical energy (from the fuel) is turned into heat when the fuel burns. The burning fuel makes the gases in the cylinder expand. This pushes the piston, giving it kinetic energy.

Valve

Spark plug

Valve

Fuel in

Cylinder

Piston

Connecting rod

Crankshaft

Oil pan

IN YOUR HOME: SEEING STARS

Do you have glow-in-the-dark stars on your bedroom ceiling? Maybe you have a glow-in-the-dark skeleton or a spider to scare people with at Halloween. Materials that glow in the dark are known as phosphorescent materials. During the day they absorb sunlight, but instead of radiating out the energy as heat, they emit the energy as light. Phosphorescent materials glow during the day, too, but we don't see it because the light they emit is much weaker than daylight.

Phosphorescent ("glow-in-the-dark") materials absorb light energy during daylight, then emit this energy again as light, rather than heat.

THE SCIENCE YOU LEARN: NEW HEAD?

In the 19th century, scientists showed that energy cannot be created or destroyed. Instead, it simply changes from one form into another. This is a basic law of physics known as the law of conservation of energy.

Engineers have known for many years that it is not possible to build a machine for transforming energy that produces more energy than is put in. In fact, engines and other machines seem to output less energy than is put in. However, careful work done by scientists in the first half of the 19th century showed that in any kind of energy transformation, energy is neither gained nor lost. The energy that seems to be "lost" in a machine has usually been turned into heat.

Only two kinds of energy

Energy seems to come in a bewildering variety of forms: heat, sound, movement, chemical energy, and many others. However, all kinds of energy are basically either kinetic energy (movement energy) or **potential energy** (stored energy). Heat energy, for example, is kinetic energy, because it is the movement of the particles in a substance. Chemical energy, on the other hand, is potential energy, because it is energy stored in the chemical bonds of a substance.

Flexible energy

The most useful type of energy to transform sunlight into is electricity. Electrical energy is extremely flexible. We can transform it easily into many other types of energy. In an electric light, for instance, the electricity is transformed into light energy by making a wire or a tube of gas glow brightly. In a hair dryer, the electricity provides the energy to turn an electric fan (kinetic energy). The electricity also flows through wires that heat up, producing heat energy.

Inside a hair dryer, air is passed over the electrically-heated wire filament (zig-zag shaped) from left to right by a fan (blue-purple, center left). This causes hot air to be blown out through the nozzle (right), which is used to dry wet hair.

In a music system the electricity is transformed into sound energy, and in a television or DVD player electricity is transformed into both sound and light. In a ski lift, electricity is used to drive motors that raise the people on the ski lift to the top of a mountain slope. In this case, the electricity is turned first into kinetic energy, then into potential energy.

Other types of energy

Electricity is a very flexible kind of energy, but you do not find electricity lying around. It has to be made from other types of energy. Most often we do this by using a turbine (a kind of fan or propeller) to turn an electric generator. The kinetic energy to turn the turbine usually comes from burning a fossil fuel (oil, gas, or coal). However, we can use other energy sources, including sunlight, to produce electricity.

THE SCIENCE YOU LEARN:
CONTROLLING THE TEMPERATURE

When William Herschel carried out his experiments on the spectrum (see page 15), he used three thermometers instead of just one. One of the thermometers measured the temperature of the light, while the other two were **controls**. They were placed close to the spectrum, but not actually in the light. The job of these two thermometers was to show up any changes in temperature that were not caused by the different colors of light. For instance, if there was a sudden draught, it might cause a drop in temperature that had nothing to do with the experiment.

Controls are an important part of any science investigation, whether in a research laboratory or at school. Without controls, it is not possible to know whether the results of an experiment are due to changes you made deliberately, or because of other changes of which you are not aware.

Energy Connections

We know that the Sun provides vital energy for all life and other processes on Earth, but how does all this happen?

Light power for plants

The green color in a plant's leaves is caused by a pigment called chlorophyll. Chlorophyll absorbs sunlight. A chemical called ATP actually captures the energy that the chlorophyll absorbs. This chemical acts as a short-term energy store. The energy stored in the ATP is used to drive a series of chemical reactions in which water (from the plant's roots) and carbon dioxide (from the air) are combined together to make sugars. This whole process is known as photosynthesis.

The sugars made in a plant's leaves provide food for the whole plant. Apart from small amounts of **minerals**, such as calcium and magnesium from the soil, the sugars are all a plant needs to survive. By harnessing the Sun's energy, plants are able to grow and reproduce.

THE SCIENCE YOU LEARN: THE WATER CYCLE

The water cycle is one of the first things we learn about the weather. This cycle is driven by the Sun's energy. Energy from sunlight warms the surface of oceans, lakes, and rivers, and causes some water to **evaporate** (become a gas). The water vapor rises into the air, and as it rises higher it gets cooler. It condenses (turns to liquid), forming tiny droplets (a cloud). Clouds are blown from place to place by the wind. Winds are also powered by energy from the Sun. If the cloud cools further, for instance as it rises over high land, the water droplets in the cloud get bigger. Instead of floating, they fall to the ground as rain or snow. Eventually, rain falling on the land drains into rivers, and then to the sea, where the whole process starts again.

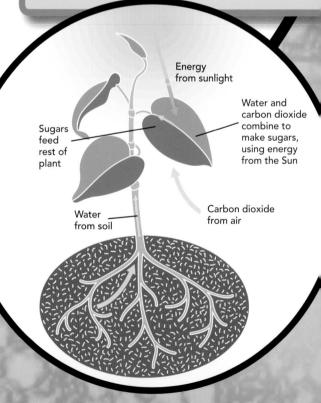

Energy from sunlight

Water and carbon dioxide combine to make sugars, using energy from the Sun

Sugars feed rest of plant

Water from soil

Carbon dioxide from air

Photosynthesis happens in a plant's leaves. Using the Sun's energy, the leaves combine carbon dioxide from the air and water from the soil to make sugars.

Food chains on land

Animals cannot make their own food. Instead, they have to eat plants or other animals to get energy. However, all this energy still comes ultimately from the Sun. The plants capture the Sun's energy in their roots, stems, leaves, flowers, and fruit. Herbivores (plant-eaters) get their energy secondhand from the plants. Most carnivores (meat-eaters) eat herbivores, so they get their Sun energy third hand. A few carnivores eat other carnivores, so their Sun energy is fourth hand.

Decomposers, such as bacteria and fungi, are creatures that break down dead and rotting animals or plants. Decomposers release simple nutrients that enrich the soil and help plants to grow. Therefore, materials from the end of the food chain feed back in at the beginning.

Food chains in the oceans

In oceans, lakes, and rivers, the Sun's energy is passed down food chains in a similar way to on land. In the ocean, the main photosynthesizers are microscopic, plant-like creatures called **algae**. They are part of the clouds of **plankton** that drift along in the ocean's currents. Every other ocean creature, from shrimps to whales, relies on the energy that these plant plankton capture from the Sun.

Herbivores get their energy from plants, which in turn get energy from the Sun. However, the plants do not change all the Sun's energy into plant material, so herbivores get less of the Sun's energy than plants.

Sun-made fuels

All plants and animals are stores of chemical potential energy. When we eat plant or animal food, we use this chemical energy to grow or to keep our bodies functioning. The chemical energy that plants make from sunlight is also the basis for fuels. Wood is the plant material most commonly used as a fuel. Wood can be turned into charcoal, which burns hotter and more cleanly than wood itself. Animal products can also be used as fuels. In places where wood is scarce, animal dung that has been dried in the Sun is traditionally used as a fuel.

The most important fuels in the modern world—oil, gas, and coal—are also stores of the Sun's energy. These fuels are called fossil fuels because they formed from plants and animals that lived millions of years ago. Coal is the fossilized remains of trees and other plants that grew in vast swamps around 300 million years ago. Oil and gas are the remains of plankton and other sea life that sank to the seabed when they died. Over time, these remains became buried and squashed. The squashing heated them up, and over many years they slowly "cooked" to form oil and gas deposits.

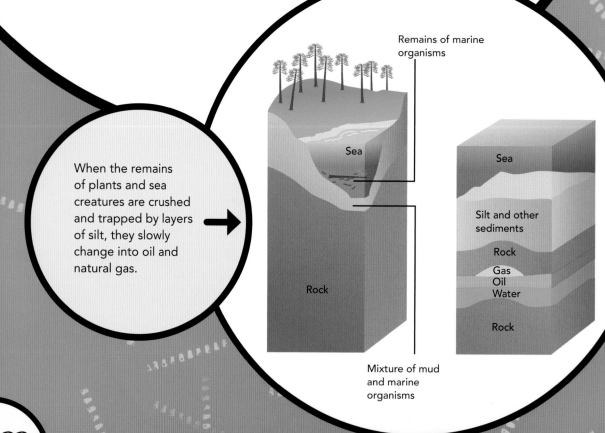

When the remains of plants and sea creatures are crushed and trapped by layers of silt, they slowly change into oil and natural gas.

Remains of marine organisms

Sea

Rock

Mixture of mud and marine organisms

Sea

Silt and other sediments

Rock

Gas
Oil
Water

Rock

"Burning Buried Sunshine"

Researcher Jeff Dukes of Utah University studied just how many ancient animals and plants are contained in fossil fuels. He calculated that more than 89 metric tons (98 tons) of fossil plant or animal material go into making just one gallon (3.8 liters) of gasoline.

The title of Dukes's 2003 research paper was "Burning Buried Sunshine." The title makes the point that fossil fuels are a vast store of solar energy, which was converted into chemical energy by living things millions of years ago, and trapped in the rocks as oil, gas, and coal deposits. However, in the processes that form oil, gas, and coal, a lot of the original energy of the plants or animals is lost. Coal contains only nine percent of the carbon in the plants it was made from. Only one part in 10,750 of the carbon from the ancient plants and animals becomes oil or gas. One gallon of gasoline (3.8 liters) contains about 4.1 kg (9 lbs) of carbon. To find the amount of carbon in the original living things the gasoline came from, Dukes multiplied his exact figure by 10,750. He then multiplied his answer by two, because only about half the weight of the original plants and animals was due to carbon. This gave him a figure of about 89,000 kg (196,000 lbs), or more than 89 metric tons (98 tons), for the weight of living things that went into making a single gallon of gasoline.

Our dependency on oil can change the appearance of our landscape, too. This massive oil pipeline runs for 1,284 km (798 miles) from the north to the south of Alaska. The pipe can transport 2 million barrels (318 million liters, or 84 million gallons) of crude oil per day.

Carbon dioxide levels

Burning fossil fuels is causing problems for the environment, because this process releases carbon dioxide that has been "locked up" in the fuel for millions of years. Burning wood for fuel does not have the same effect. This is because the trees that the wood comes from take carbon dioxide from the atmosphere. When the wood is burned, this carbon dioxide is released back into the atmosphere. As long as new trees are planted to replace the old ones, burning wood is carbon neutral. This means that it does not add to the overall levels of carbon dioxide in the atmosphere.

Biofuels

Wood is a type of **biofuel**. Biofuels are made from plant or animal materials. Modern vehicles and power plants cannot run on wood, and it would be impossible to grow forests quickly enough to meet the world's huge energy demands. However, other kinds of biofuel could make better replacements for fossil fuels. In South America and the United States, the most popular biofuel is ethanol (alcohol). This can be used in ordinary cars as a substitute for gasoline (it is most often used in a mixture with gasoline). Brazil is the world's biggest producer of ethanol.

There are stations selling biodiesel across Europe. However, there are not many, and the fuel is sometimes blended with ordinary diesel. Biodiesel-blend pumps also can be found around the United States.

Cars have been running on ethanol made from sugar cane since the 1970s. Most cars in Brazil run on a gasoline mixture that is at least 25% ethanol. In the United States, ethanol is made mostly from soybeans or corn. Large amounts of ethanol are made, but it is mostly added in small quantities to gasoline rather than being used as a fuel in its own right.

In Europe, biodiesel is the main biofuel. Biodiesel can be made from many types of plant oil, or from used cooking oil. A third type of biofuel is biogas. This can be made by **fermenting** animal wastes and some types of garbage in special reactors. Fermenting is a process that involves mixing the material with bacteria or other microbes in a sealed container with no air.

Rocket stoves

Fuels like wood or animal dung are usually burned on open fires. This type of fire is not very efficient—much of the heat from the fuel is wasted. In some less economically developed countries, a fuel-efficient stove, called a rocket stove, has been developed. This stove uses much less fuel for cooking and heating, which saves time gathering or preparing fuel, and gives people more time for other tasks, such as growing food.

Another more efficient way of using simple biofuels, such as wood, is in a biomass furnace. This very efficient furnace can be used to power the central heating for large buildings. It is designed to burn wood chips or pellets of compressed sawdust. These are fuels made from materials that are usually waste products.

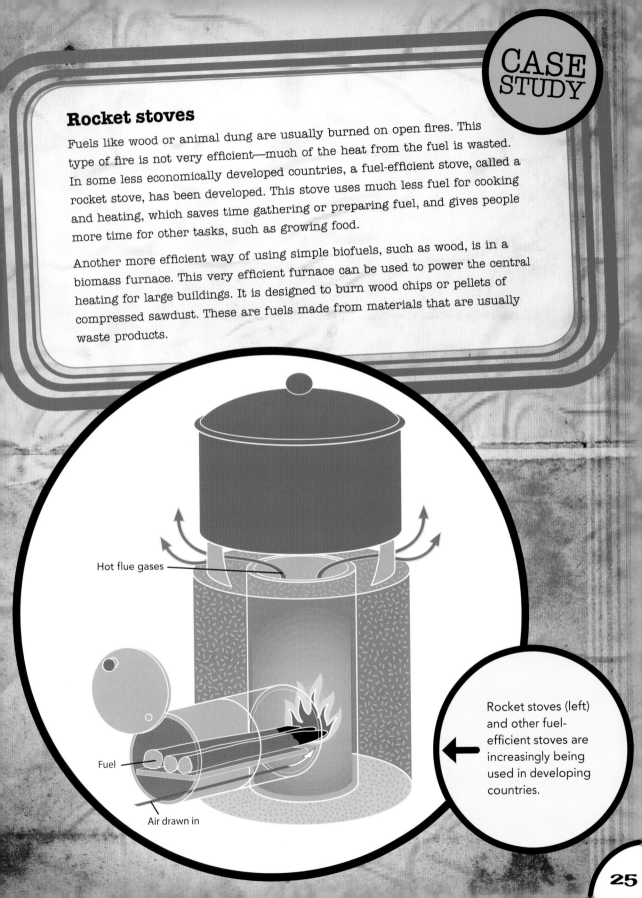

Hot flue gases

Fuel

Air drawn in

Rocket stoves (left) and other fuel-efficient stoves are increasingly being used in developing countries.

Biofuel worries

Although many countries are starting to produce biofuels on a large scale, there are many problems still to be solved. It takes a lot of energy to grow crops like corn and rapeseed. Farmers need to use fertilizers and weed killers to grow the crops, and farm machinery like tractors to plant and harvest them. This means that biofuels made from these crops do still add to climate change, although less so than fossil fuels. There are also worries that crops grown for fuel will take over areas of forest land, leading to deforestation and destruction of wildlife habitats and farmland previously used for food. In poor countries this could lead to many people starving.

This field of corn in the United States could be turned into biofuel at the refinery in the background. Corn is widely used in the United States to make bioethanol. However, it is a poor crop to use, because large amounts of energy are used to grow the crop.

These bacteria have been genetically modified so that they can make bioethanol from just about any type of plant material.

Biofuels for the future?

Several groups of researchers are investigating how to make biofuels from microbes, rather than from plants. The main advantage is that the microbes could grow virtually anywhere, and there would not be competition between land for growing food, and land for producing biofuels.

One possibility is to make biodiesel from microscopic, plant-like algae. Algae are found in most watery environments. Some types of algae have a high oil content, and several groups of scientists have been researching how to grow large amounts of the algae and extract the oil to make biodiesel. Other researchers are investigating using algae to produce hydrogen gas, and some bacteria have been successfully **genetically modified** to produce gasoline. All these techniques could be useful in the future, but at present they are small scale and cost more than producing fuel by other methods.

The United States uses more gasoline and diesel fuel than any other country. Michael Briggs, a scientist at the University of New Hampshire, calculated how much biodiesel would be needed to replace all the United States's current gasoline and diesel consumption. He then worked out that algae farms covering a total of 38,850 sq km (15,000 sq miles) would be needed to produce this amount of biodiesel. This sounds like a large area, but in fact it is only one-eighth of the area of the Sonora Desert in California.

Other energy sources

As well as being the basis of life, energy from the Sun powers many natural processes on Earth. On page 14 we saw how the uneven heating of different parts of Earth causes winds in Earth's atmosphere. Uneven heating also causes the oceans close to the Equator to be heated more than the oceans at the North and South Poles. The result is that convection currents carry warmer water away from the Equator. The spinning motion of Earth causes the water to travel in giant circular movements, called gyres, rather than moving directly away from the Equator.

The warmth of the Sun also causes water to evaporate from the oceans, lakes, and rivers. This is the start of the water cycle, in which water rises up into the air, then falls to Earth again as rain or snow.

Hydroelectricity

All these Sun-powered processes also offer alternative sources of energy to fossil fuels. Hydroelectricity (generating electricity from running water) is the oldest type of alternative energy. About seven percent of all the world's electricity is produced this way. Hydroelectric power is cheap and reliable, but most of the world's best hydroelectric sites already have hydroelectric power plants.

Wind power

Wind power is a growing source of electric power. Wind turbines are turned by the wind blowing over them. The turning propeller turns an electric generator. Many countries are building wind farms to generate energy. Wind power is also cheap and clean, but there are relatively few places where there is a good wind for most of the year. One solution to this may be to build offshore wind farms. Another could be to build wind turbines that can fly, using the propeller-like turbine to give them lift as well as turning the generator. These turbines can be fastened by a long cable at a height of 11 km (7 miles). At this height the turbines would be flying in the **jet stream**, where a strong wind blows all year round.

Tidal generators

There are few large power stations that harness the energy of the waves or the tides. One new idea that may be promising is the tidal stream generator. This is an underwater propeller that gets energy from the movement of water as the tide flows in and out. Tidal stream generators are still very new, but they look likely to have a promising future.

In this hydroelectric power plant near Essen, Germany, the power of the Ruhr River is used to turn electric generators. Even after it has flowed through the power plant, the water still has plenty of energy.

Energy Direct

We have seen that most of our energy sources—fossil fuels, moving water, wind, and others—owe their energy originally to the Sun. However, it would be much better if we could use the Sun's energy directly. If we could gather all the sunlight that falls on Earth in just one minute, it would provide more energy than the world uses in one year.

Solar homes

People have been using the Sun's energy directly for many years. Ancient peoples often aligned their homes so that the Sun warmed them. For hundreds of years, houses in the Middle East have been built with walls that keep out the Sun during the day, and then release the Sun's warmth into the building during the night. Greenhouses are another simple way in which people have used the Sun's heat for centuries.

Greenhouses trap the Sun's heat, which keeps the greenhouse warmer than its surroundings during the day. Greenhouses can be used to grow plants that would not survive in a cool climate.

CUTTING EDGE: THE PHOTOELECTRIC EFFECT

It is possible to capture the Sun's energy and convert it directly into electricity. This is called the photoelectric effect. It happens when a metal is exposed to light or other radiation. The atoms in the metal absorb energy from the radiation, and this causes them to release **electrons**. The release of electrons produces an electric current, because electricity is produced by moving electrons. Light is only one of many kinds of radiation, ranging from radio waves to X-rays, so not all metals produce electricity in response to light radiation. The photoelectric effect is the basis for solar cells, which produce electricity when light falls on them. The strength of the effect depends on what metal, or combination of metals, is used.

Solar heating

It was not until the 19th century that anyone used the Sun's power to do useful work. In 1865, a French mathematics teacher, Auguste Mouchout, built a small, solar-powered steam engine. He used a reflector to concentrate sunlight on a cauldron of water, which was heated to become steam. Mouchout's engine was never fully developed, because cheap coal became available and was used as the main fuel for steam engines.

Other inventors soon came up with ideas for concentrating the Sun's energy. In 1870, Swedish-American engineer John Ericsson (1803–1889) built a steam engine using a reflector in the shape of a trough, with a pipe running down the center of it. In 1879, a British government official in India, William Adams, built a circular array of flat mirrors focused on a boiler at the center. In 1885, French engineer Charles Tellier (1828–1913) built a flat solar panel that heated the water flowing through it. All four of these methods for focusing the Sun's energy have been used since the 1980s to build solar power plants.

Sunlight to electricity

In 1839, French scientist Alexandre-Edmond Becquerel was the first person to observe the photoelectric effect. In 1873, British electrical engineer Willoughby Smith accidentally discovered that the **element** selenium produces electricity when it is exposed to light. In 1884, American inventor Charles Fritts made the first working solar cell using selenium. The cell had an **efficiency** of less than one percent (it turned less than one percent of the light falling on the cell into electricity), so it was not widely used. However, selenium cells did find a use in the light meters of cameras.

It was not until 1954 that a practical solar cell was first made. This was developed at Bell Laboratories in the United States. The efficiency of the earliest cells was six percent, but this improved quickly. By 1958 it had reached 10 percent, and by 1960 it was 14 percent. Solar cells were now workable, but very expensive!

The first silicon solar cell was discovered by Russell Ohls (1898–1987), who worked at Bell Laboratories. While testing a slice of silicon with a crack down the middle, he noticed that it produced electricity when it was in the light, but not in the dark.

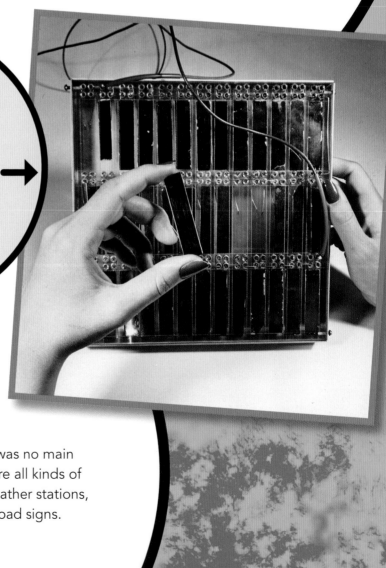

As solar cells were used more and more, they got better and cheaper. One early use in the 1970s was in solar-powered calculators. Solar power was also used for electrical devices in isolated places, where there was no main electricity supply. Today there are all kinds of solar-powered devices, from weather stations, to emergency telephones and road signs.

CUTTING EDGE:
SOLAR CELLS IN SPACE

Solar cells were first used in spacecraft. The satellite *Vanguard I*, launched in 1958, was the first spacecraft to be solar powered. It was a scientific research satellite, full of sensitive instruments. Today, satellites, space probes, and the International Space Station all use solar panels (arrays of solar cells) to provide electricity. In space there are no clouds to block the Sun. The solar panels produce electricity throughout the day, and charge up batteries to keep the equipment running overnight.

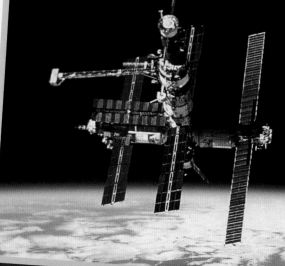

The *Mir* space station was one of many spacecraft that used large solar panels to generate electricity.

CASE STUDY

Using solar power to save vaccines

In less economically developed countries, many lives can be saved by vaccinating children against certain diseases. Vaccinations need to be kept cold until they are used, or they quickly lose their effectiveness. Keeping vaccines cool in rural areas can be difficult when there is no electricity supply. One solution that has been developed in recent years is to use solar-powered refrigerators. One type of solar fridge was developed by the World Health Organization. During the day, solar power provides enough electricity to keep the fridge working and to build up a supply of ice. At night, the fridge does not work, but the ice supply keeps the vaccines cold until morning.

Cutting electricity costs

Using solar cells and solar panels can reduce a building's electricity costs. Solar panels fitted to the building can supply all or part of the electricity needs. The initial cost of installing the panels is quite high—currently it takes at least 10 years before solar panels earn back the money they cost to install. However, many scientists and **environmentalists** say that governments should provide grants to install solar panels, because this would speed up the changeover to cleaner sources of energy.

Solar panels are usually connected to the main electric grid by a device called a grid inverter. If the panels produce more electricity than is needed, the extra flows through the meter the other way, and feeds electricity into the main.

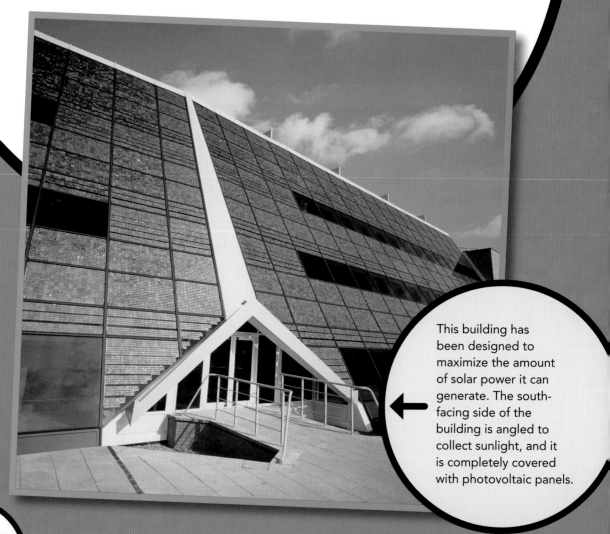

This building has been designed to maximize the amount of solar power it can generate. The south-facing side of the building is angled to collect sunlight, and it is completely covered with photovoltaic panels.

Solar vehicles

The first solar-powered "car" was built by Briton Alan Freeman in 1979. By the mid-1980s, solar car races were held, and in 1989 the first World Solar Challenge race took place. This was a race of 3,021 km (1,877 miles) across central Australia, from Darwin to Adelaide.

The first solar-powered aircraft was *Gossamer Penguin*, built by American Paul MacCready (1925–2007), which flew in 1980. In 1981, an improved design called *Solar Challenger* flew 262 km (163 miles) from Paris, France, to Manston, UK. Later, unmanned solar aircraft included *Pathfinder*, *Centurion*, and *Helios*.

The solar aircraft *Helios* had a wingspan bigger than that of a jumbo jet. It flew successfully for two years, but crashed in 2003.

CUTTING EDGE: SOLAR BOATS

The first solar-powered boat was built before the first solar car, in 1975. Today there are many boats operating commercially that work at least partly on solar power. In 1996, Japanese sailor Ken'ichi Horie sailed across the Pacific Ocean in his solar-powered boat *Malt's Mermaid*. In 2007, a solar-powered Swiss catamaran called *Sun21* crossed the Atlantic Ocean.

Solar power plants

In recent years, governments in several countries have encouraged the building of solar power plants. Japan and Germany, in particular, have increased the number of solar power plants they have.

In a solar thermal power plant, electricity is generated by concentrating heat from the Sun and using the heat to produce steam or gas. This is used to power a steam turbine or a gas turbine, which turns an electric generator.

Most solar power plants use solar panels to generate electricity directly from sunlight. In theory this should be the most efficient way to get electricity from sunlight. However, in practice, solar panels are not as efficient on a large scale as solar heating power plants. Solar heating power plants all use a collector (a mirror of some kind) to focus the Sun's rays onto a receiver, which gets hot. The differences are in the shapes of the different collectors.

Three kinds of solar heating power plant have been developed, each one collecting and focusing the heat in a different way. **Parabolic** (dish-like) collectors are the most efficient at focusing the Sun's heat, but they are also the most expensive to make. Collecting sunlight using arrays of flat mirrors is cheapest, but least efficient. Trough collectors are between the two.

Although there have been large increases in solar power generation in recent years, solar power still supplies only a tiny fraction of the world's total energy. Sunlight itself is free, but solar power plants cost a lot to build and run, so solar energy is expensive. However, costs are falling as technology improves, and more power plants are built. In the future we are likely to produce far more electricity using solar power.

Solar thermal power plants

In a solar thermal power plants, electricity is generated by concentrating heat from the Sun and using the heat to produce steam or gas. This is used to power a steam turbine or a gas turbine, which turns an electric generator.

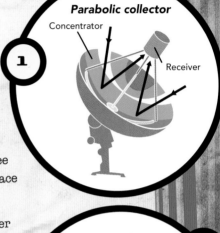

Parabolic collector

Concentrator

Receiver

1

The first large solar thermal power plants did not produce electricity, but were solar furnaces producing steel. They are both in the Pyrenees Mountains in France. The largest, at Odeillo, uses Mouchout's idea (see page 31) of a giant parabolic (dished) mirror to focus sunlight onto a furnace (see diagram 1). The sunlight heats the iron in the furnace to a temperature of 3,000°C (5,430°F).

Another type of solar power plant is the solar power tower (see diagram 2). This is based on Adams's idea of using an array of flat mirrors to focus sunlight on one point. The focal point in this case is the top of a tall tower. Solar power towers have been built in the United States and in Spain. The Spanish PS10 tower, near Seville, is part of a complex of solar generators that will eventually produce 300 megawatts (MW) of power. This is enough electricity to supply over 100,000 homes.

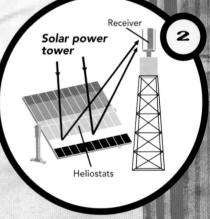

Receiver

Solar power tower

2

Heliostats

A third type of solar thermal power plant uses Tellier's idea of a long, curved trough mirror to focus sunlight on a pipe running along the bottom of the mirror (see diagram 3). In the Mojave Desert in California, a group of seven SEGS (Solar Electricity Generating System) power plants all use trough collectors to generate electricity. Together they produce over 350 MW of electricity, making the SEGS complex the biggest solar power plant in the world.

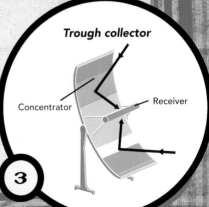

Trough collector

Concentrator

Receiver

3

Energy for the Future?

In the future, we want to use less fossil fuel and more clean, renewable energy sources. Recent advances in research, and improvements in old ideas, suggest that in the future solar power could be an important source of this clean energy.

Nanotechnology has made it possible to make flexible plastic solar panels like this one.

CUTTING EDGE: NANOTECHNOLOGY

A nanometer (nm) is one-billionth of one meter (3.3 ft.). A single human hair is about 8,000 nm wide. Nanotechnology is engineering on a nanometer scale, which is the scale of atoms and molecules. Usually this involves using very carefully controlled chemical processes. Scientists have used nanotechnology to make incredibly tiny wires and tubes, gears, motors, and even a "car" that is just 4 nm long. Twenty thousand such cars could be parked on the tip of a human hair.

Spray-on energy

In the past, solar panels were too expensive and not efficient enough to provide a practical source of electricity. However, research around the world has made gradual improvements. Today, solar power is on the edge of a breakthrough. Researchers at universities and in energy companies worldwide are putting effort and money into solar energy research, to try and improve the design and reduce the cost of solar panels.

Today's solar panels are heavy and rigid, and the very pure silicon needed to make them is in short supply. However, new

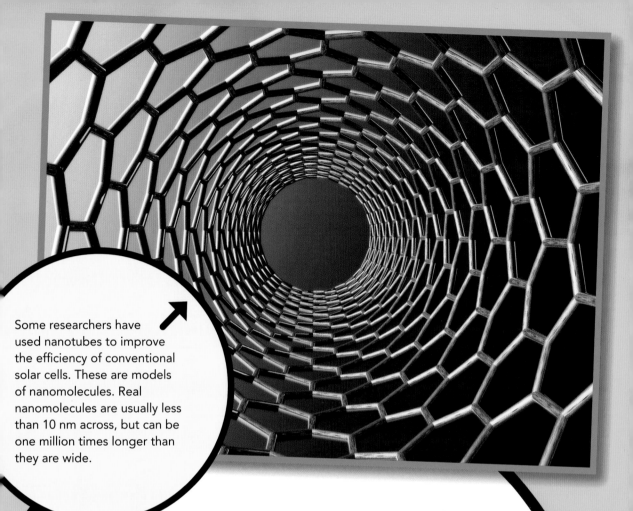

Some researchers have used nanotubes to improve the efficiency of conventional solar cells. These are models of nanomolecules. Real nanomolecules are usually less than 10 nm across, but can be one million times longer than they are wide.

materials could revolutionize solar cells. These materials are made using nanoparticles. Nanoparticles are extremely tiny balls, tubes, or fibers. Researchers have found that by adding nanoparticles to a solar cell, they can make it almost twice as efficient (the panel can produce twice as much electricity from a fixed amount of light). Solar nanoparticles can also be used to extend the range of radiation that the solar cell can absorb. For example, the cell could be made to convert infrared radiation into electricity as well as visible light.

Solar cells containing nanoparticles can be made on a flexible plastic base material. This makes them lighter, more flexible, and cheaper to produce than normal solar cells. Currently, flexible solar cells are not as efficient as conventional ones. However, with so much research happening worldwide, it should not be long before we have cheap, flexible, and efficient solar cells. It should even be possible to produce "solar paint," which can be painted onto surfaces, such as roof tiles or car bodies.

Solar towers

Another way of producing power from the Sun on a large scale could be to use solar towers. Architects who want a low-energy way to cool buildings often use solar chimneys. These are chimneys taller than the building, with openings into the building lower down and an opening to the outside at the top. Warm air from inside the building rises up the chimneys and out into the surroundings, creating a cooling breeze through the building.

A solar tower works in a similar way, but on a larger scale. At the center is a tall, hollow tower. This is surrounded by a solar collector, which is similar to a huge, low greenhouse. Around the tower base, where the collector connects to it, are a ring of wind turbines.

During the day, sunlight heats up the air inside the solar collector. The hot air is light, and it is drawn up the central tower. This creates a strong wind that turns the turbines at the base of the tower. The design includes plastic tubes filled with water inside the solar collector. These store heat during the day while the Sun is on them. At night the water tubes emit their stored energy, which keeps the wind generators running during the night.

THE SCIENCE YOU LEARN: AIR DENSITY

In school we learn about convection currents. When air is warmed it expands, becomes less dense, and rises. An air flow begins as cooler air moves in to replace the rising air.

The solar tower relies on the fact that air rises when it is warmed. You can see this expansion happen before your eyes when a hot-air balloon is being set up. At first the balloon is just a huge, flat piece of fabric, with a hoop and a gas burner at one end. When the gas burner is turned on, the fabric begins to billow and ripple. Gradually, it fills up with air, and then the whole thing rises slowly off the ground. Eventually the balloon has to be held down with ropes and pegs to prevent it from flying away.

Why does air expand and becomes less dense as it gets warmer? It happens because as air gets warmer, the particles that it is made from gain more energy and move faster. This makes them spread out more.

Solar towers are a fairly untested type of solar power, but the technology is fairly simple and, once built, should operate at a low cost. There are plans to build a large solar tower in Spain, and an even larger one in Australia. If these are successful, they could be the start of a new way to harness the Sun's energy.

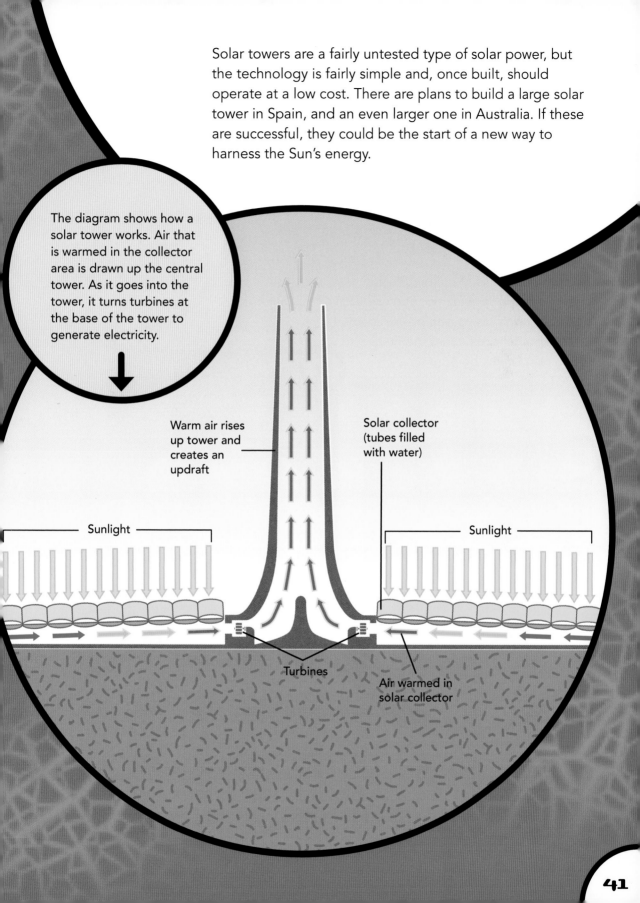

The diagram shows how a solar tower works. Air that is warmed in the collector area is drawn up the central tower. As it goes into the tower, it turns turbines at the base of the tower to generate electricity.

Warm air rises up tower and creates an updraft

Solar collector (tubes filled with water)

Sunlight

Sunlight

Turbines

Air warmed in solar collector

Fusing atoms

The Sun produces energy by a process called nuclear fusion. Could we do the same thing here on Earth?

In nuclear fusion, the nuclei (centers) of hydrogen atoms crash into each other so hard that they fuse (join together). The joined hydrogen nuclei are now a different substance called helium. When hydrogen atoms fuse in this way, they release an enormous amount of energy—much more than we get from existing nuclear power plants.

Two different ways of building fusion reactors are currently being researched, one using magnetic fields, the other using lasers (see box on page 43). Scientists are hopeful that the first fusion reactor will be operating by 2016.

1 Lasers heat a pellet of fuel. The outer layers explode outward.

2 The explosion compresses the center of the fuel pellet, and another laser heats it even more.

3 The combination of heat and pressure causes fusion.

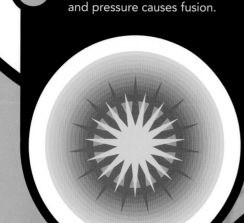

If we can make fusion work, it could provide enormous amounts of energy from very little fuel. However, building fusion reactors is proving to be extremely expensive, and progress is slow. Most experts believe it could be 50 years or more before fusion reactors really contribute to energy production.

Discovery of Fusion

The person who first suggested how the Sun and other stars get their energy was German-American scientist Hans Bethe (1905–2005). He had studied all the nuclear reactions that were known to take place, and in 1938 he showed that two of these reactions explained how the Sun and other stars got their energy. One reaction, which only happens in very large, brilliant stars, involves hydrogen and carbon. The other, which takes place in the Sun and other smaller stars, is fusion. Bethe's discoveries revolutionized the study of the stars, and in 1967 he was awarded a Nobel Prize for his work.

CUTTING EDGE: TOKAMAKS AND LASERS

After World War II, researchers took the first step toward developing a fusion reactor, which was to find a way of containing gases at very high temperatures (these gases are called plasmas). A plasma hot enough for fusion to happen would melt any kind of container it was put in. However, plasmas are electrically charged, so researchers developed a way of containing plasma using magnetic fields. In 1968, Russian scientists Igor Tamm (1895–1971) and Andrei Sakharov (1921–1989) built a magnetic containment device shaped like a hollow doughnut. They called it a tokamak. This has been the basis for all magnetic fusion reactors ever since.

Meanwhile, another fusion device was being developed. In 1960, the first lasers were built. Researchers from several countries worked out that very powerful lasers could in theory be used to contain a small amount of fusion material, heat it to a high temperature, and compress it.

Since the 1960s, scientists have been building ever more powerful tokamaks and lasers, so that they can heat hydrogen to higher temperatures and compress it with greater pressures. Scientists can now produce temperatures of more than 500 million°C (900 million°F). This is more than 50 times higher than the temperature at the heart of the Sun! Researchers have managed to achieve fusion for very short times, but the process uses slightly more energy than it produces.

Working at such incredible temperatures, right on the frontiers of science, involves very expensive equipment. Fusion research is now an international effort, because few countries can afford to build their own tokamaks and lasers. Currently an enormous tokamak called ITER is being built in southern France, which should be in operation by 2016. Two powerful new laser fusion plants are also being built, one in the United States and one in Europe.

Future transportation

Solar-powered boats have already been proven to work, and practical cars and aircraft have been built. In the future it seems likely that all these forms of transportation will be further developed. With thin, flexible, nanoparticle solar coatings, it will be possible to cover all the upper surfaces of solar-powered vehicles without affecting the shape. Lightweight, solar-powered aircraft will be able to circle the world without needing to refuel. However, it is likely that many vehicles will be **hybrids**, combining solar power with fuel cells or some other form of power. This is necessary to supplement the solar power at night, for instance.

Major car manufacturers are developing new technologies for vehicles that can run on fuel cells, or a combination of fuel cells and solar energy. In this photo, a hydrogen fuel cell vehicle fills up at a hydrogen station in the United States.

In the future there are likely to be new uses for solar power in space. A group of scientists working in Switzerland are planning a Mars space mission that would involve the use of an unmanned, solar-powered aircraft. Unlike a ground-based vehicle, an aircraft could cover a large area of ground in a fairly short time, and it would show the ground in more detail than when viewed from a satellite. Solar power would allow the aircraft to fly for long periods without having to transport heavy fuel to Mars.

CUTTING EDGE: SOLAR SAILS

The Sun may also aid a new kind of space travel in the near future, in the form of solar sails. These are an idea first suggested in the early 20th century. A large, very lightweight sail spread out in space would make it possible to move a spacecraft along using light itself. Although it is hard to believe, the light from the Sun can actually act in the same way as the wind on Earth. It can push a solar sail spacecraft along. At first the spacecraft will move slowly, but it could eventually reach speeds of 324,000 kph (201,300 mph), over ten times faster than the space shuttle.

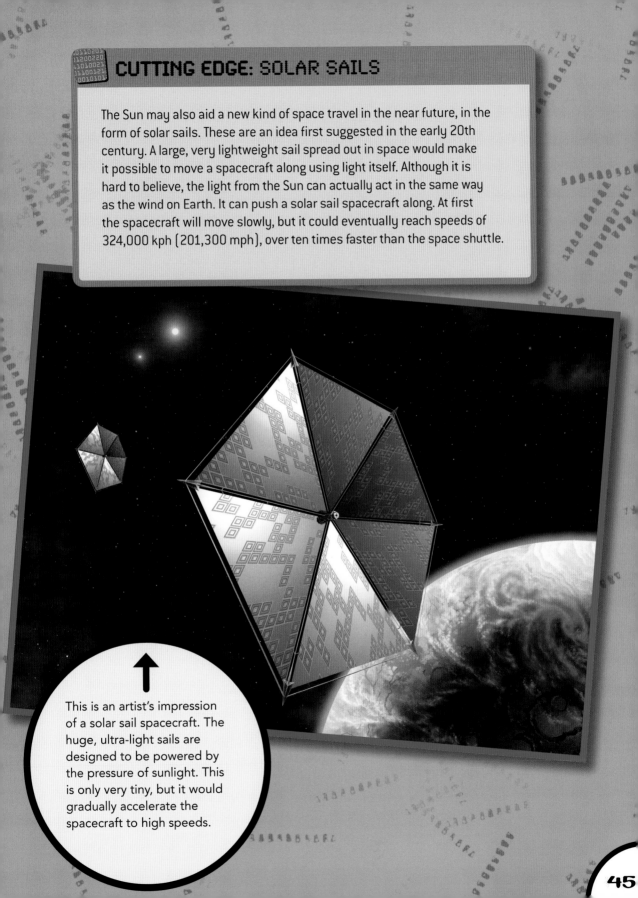

This is an artist's impression of a solar sail spacecraft. The huge, ultra-light sails are designed to be powered by the pressure of sunlight. This is only very tiny, but it would gradually accelerate the spacecraft to high speeds.

Conclusion

Harnessing the Sun's energy is not just about turning light into electricity. Plants, animals, weather, and ocean currents all exist because of the energy that pours out of the Sun. If we follow the energy trail backward, we find that most of our sources of energy—fossil fuels, biofuels, wind power, hydroelectric power, and of course solar power—also come from the Sun. Events on the Sun can quickly affect us on Earth, even though the Sun is 150 million km (93 million miles) away. A solar flare produces storms of protons that affect electronic equipment on Earth. Variation in the number of sunspots affects Earth's climate.

The PS 10 solar heating power station in Seville, Spain. This kind of solar power station offers the hope of clean solar energy for the future.

CUTTING EDGE: HOW SCIENCE HELPS

Science has played an essential part in helping us to understand how much we rely on the Sun's energy. It is amazing to think that simple processes like convection and radiation are happening at incredibly high temperatures, and on a massive scale, inside the Sun. At the other end of the scale, the tiny atoms and molecules that we learn about in science smash into each other in the center of the Sun, producing huge amounts of energy.

Science has also been essential to the process of harnessing the Sun's energy on Earth. Again and again we find that scientific investigations, which seemed obscure when they were made, are behind inventions and discoveries that have brought improvements to our lives. For example, French scientist Alexandre-Edmond Becquerel was studying phosphorescence (a kind of glow emitted by some materials) in compounds of uranium and sulphur. In doing so, he discovered the photoelectric effect that eventually led to solar cells.

Not straightforward

When practical solar cells were first developed in the 1950s, people imagined that it would not be long before everything ran on solar power, and that we would have endless amounts of cheap energy. In practice, turning light directly into electricity is not a straightforward solution to our energy problems. Although the energy itself is free, the equipment for capturing the Sun's energy has proven to be expensive. Large-scale solar power plants are especially expensive to build and maintain.

However, with recent improvements in efficiency and the development of plastic solar cells, we could be on the verge of a solar revolution. Solar cells may prove to be most useful on the small scale, providing built-in power for individual devices and buildings. Other ways of harnessing sunlight, such as wind and wave power, solar towers, and solar thermal power plants, can be used for producing energy on a large scale.

In the longer term, we may get our energy from fusion, the process that gives the Sun its energy in the first place. Whatever solutions we find for shortages of fossil fuels and the problems of climate change, there is no doubt that one way or another, the energy will come from the Sun.

Facts and Figures

Sun fact file

Mass	1,989 billion billion billion kg (4,385 billion billion billion lbs)
Radius	695,000 km (432,200 miles)
Rotational period	25–36 days
Average surface temperature	6,000°C (10,830°F)
Temperature at core	15 million°C (27 million°F)
Age	4.5 billion years

Main chemical components
  Hydrogen
  Helium
	
	92.1 percent
	7.8 percent

- The Sun is 332,830 times heavier than Earth. About 98 percent of the total mass of the solar system is in the Sun.
- The radius of the Sun is 109 times that of Earth. Its total volume is equivalent to about 1.3 million Earths.
- Light from the Sun takes eight minutes to reach Earth.
- The Sun is exactly the right age, distance, temperature, and brightness for life to exist on Earth.
- The Sun is almost halfway through its life, and at its most stable.
- Sunshine provides human beings with our main source of vitamin D. This vitamin strengthens our bones and muscles and boosts the immune system.

Topics to research

- Is solar power being used in your area? Do some research and see if there is a solar power plant near you. Are there any buildings with solar panels on the roof? What about solar-powered road signs?

- Can people get grants if they want to put solar panels on their roofs? The best place to look for this information might be an association of solar energy. For instance, the Solar Energy Industries Association (SEIA) at www.seia.org.

- Who are the scientists researching solar power? Can you find out which scientists are at the cutting edge of research? Can you find any examples of universities working with commercial companies, sharing research and ideas?

- The World Solar Challenge is sponsored by an oil company, Shell. Are they doing any research into solar-powered vehicles or solar power? What about other oil companies? Are any car manufacturers developing solar-powered cars?

Solar energy timeline

1838	French scientist Alexandre-Edmond Becquerel first observes the photoelectric effect.
1860–81	Frenchman Auguste Mouchout designs a device that turns solar energy into steam power.
1873	British electrical engineer Willoughby Smith discovers that the metal selenium produces an electric current when exposed to light.
1884	American inventor Charles Fritts builds the first working solar cell. However, his solar cell has an efficiency of only between one and two percent.
1916	American physicist Robert Millikan provides experimental proof of the photoelectric effect.
1923	German physicist Albert Einstein receives the Nobel Prize for his explanation of the photoelectric effect.
1954	Bell Laboratories make the first practical solar panel, with an efficiency of six percent.
1956	The first commercial solar cell goes on sale, but cost is $300 per watt.
1958	The satellite *Vanguard I* is the first satellite to use solar energy to generate electricity.
1950s–60s	Many space vehicles use solar power to generate electricity.
1970s	Renewed interest in solar energy as oil crisis leads to rising oil and gas prices. Price of solar cells drops dramatically to about $20 per watt.
1972	Solar power is first used for applications on Earth. The French install a solar-powered system in a village school in Niger, Africa, to run a television for education.
1980	First solar-powered aircraft, *Gossamer Penguin*, is built by American Paul MacCready. An improved design, *Solar Challenger*, follows in 1981.
1982	Worldwide solar power production is only 9.3 MW, but growing fast. By 1983 it is more than 21 MW.

1985	Researchers at the University of New South Wales, Australia, build a solar cell that is more than 20 percent efficient.
1989	First World Solar Challenge race is held. The race Is 3,021 km (1,877 miles) across central Australia, from Darwin to Adelaide.
1994	The National Renewable Energy Laboratory in the United States develops the first solar cell to exceed 30 percent efficiency.
1996	Solar Two, a test 10 MW solar concentrator begins to operate.
2001	American solar aircraft, *Helios*, developed by NASA from *Solar Challenger* design, reaches a world height record of almost 30,000 m (98,430 ft.).
2002–03	Several large solar power plants built in Germany. World's largest photovoltaic plant, at Hemau near Regensburg, begins operating.
2005	Researchers from New Mexico State University and Wake Forest University develop the first practical flexible solar cell. Efficiency is only 5.25 percent, but improving rapidly.

Find Out More

Books

Anderson, Lorraine and Rick Palkovic. *Cooking with Sunshine: The Complete Guide to Solar Cuisine with 150 Easy Sun-Cooked Recipes.* New York: Da Capo Press, 2006.
Contains advice on how to cook using the Sun's energy, without solar panels or generators.

Clarke, Arthur C. *The Wind from the Sun.* London: Orion, 1990.
A science fiction short story book. In one story, called *Sunjammer,* a spaceship designer builds a sun yacht with a solar sail powered by light.

Graham, Ian. *Discovering Space: The Sun.* Mankato, Minn.: Black Rabbit Books, 2007.

Raum, Elizabeth. *Potato Clocks and Solar Cars: Renewable and Nonrenewable Energy.* Chicago: Raintree, 2007.

Royston, Angela. *The Day the Sun Went Out: The Sun's Energy.* Chicago: Raintree, 2005.

Websites

- www.windows.ucar.edu/tour/link=/Sun/Sun.html
  Learn more about the interior of the Sun, activity on the
  Sun's surface, and much more.

- http://ds9.ssl.berkeley.edu/viewer/flash/flash.html
  Look at today's view of the Sun, a diagram of the structure
  of the Sun, a film of a solar flare, and much more.

- www.jet.efda.org/pages/fusion-basics.html
  A simple explanation of how tokamak fusion works, from
  the JET Laboratory, UK, one of the leading fusion
  research centers.

- http://news.bbc.co.uk/2/hi/science/nature/default.stm
  A good place to look for simply written, short news stories about
  new developments in solar energy.

- www.nrel.gov/solar/
  Find out about research into solar power in the United States on
  the website of the National Renewable Energy Laboratory.

Glossary

alga (plural is algae) plant-like living thing found mostly in water. Many algae are microscopic, but seaweeds are also algae.

atom very tiny particle that makes up every object in the universe

biofuel fuel made from plant or animal materials

climate change any long-term, significant changes in average temperatures, weather patterns, or wind direction

control "blank" experiment run alongside a scientific experiment to show any variables that have not been taken into account

convection transfer of heat from one place to another by currents moving through a liquid or gas

density how heavy something is compared to the amount of space it takes up

efficiency the proportion of energy put into a machine or other device that is converted into useful energy

electron very tiny particle that forms the outer part of atoms. Electrons have a negative charge.

element substance made of only one type of atom. Carbon, oxygen, calcium, and metals like iron and aluminium are common elements.

environmentalist someone who is concerned about the negative impact that human life has on the environment and is looking for ways to prevent further damage

evaporate turn from liquid into gas

fermenting growing microbes in conditions where they have little or no air

fossil fuel oil, gas, or coal

genetically modified when a living thing has genes from another living thing added to it

hybrid vehicle that has more than one kind of power system. Most hybrid vehicles have both a gasoline or diesel engine and an electric motor.

industrialized type of place where most people live in cities and work in factories or offices, rather than as farmers

infrared type of electromagnetic energy; heat radiation

jet stream fast-flowing band of air currents located around 10–15 kilometers (6–9 miles) above Earth's surface

kinetic energy energy of movement

mineral simple substance found in rocks or in the ground, usually obtained by mining

nuclear fusion nuclear reaction that happens in the Sun in which two hydrogen atoms come together (fuse) to form helium

nuclear reaction reaction that involves the nucleus (central part) of an atom. In chemical reactions, atoms combine and split apart, but they are not changed themselves. In a nuclear reaction atoms change from one kind to another.

parabolic curved or dish-like in shape

plankton tiny creatures that live in the ocean and drift with its currents

potential energy stored energy

solar flare explosion on the Sun's surface that sends jets of flaming gas thousands of miles into space

spectrum range of color formed when a beam of white light is dispersed, as through a prism, so that the wavelengths are arranged in order

thermogram image produced by a thermographic camera that can detect radiation. The thermogram shows the variations in temperature of an object or place.

wavelength distance between two peaks of a wave. Light and other similar kinds of radiation are energy waves. Light has a wavelength between 400 and 650 nanometers.

Index